Reach Out in the Darkness:

How Pop Music Saved My Mortal Soul

Jim Farfaglia

Clearpath Publishing
Fulton, New York
Copyright 2014 by Jim Farfaglia
All rights reserved
Printed in the United States of America

Cover art by Joe Abbate

ISBN: 978-1500940317

To Julie

*Sometimes we think a person comes into our life
for one reason,
but it turns out to be, very much,
for another.*

Contents

Contents

side A

The Old Songs

To the 45, Thanks

for the easy way you let me in:
your open door of catchy melodies
and your right-as-rain lyrics

were just what I needed
to escape a headed-for-disaster life
on this side of vinyl;

so lucky to catch a ride
with the perfect you
         spinning

the kind of world I could live in.

Raised

James
singing his sweet baby lullaby

John
reminding us that all we need is love

Art & Paul
weaving their sounds of silence

Carole
making the earth move...

The voices from my bedside radio,
rising above the breaking news
and clever chatter

as I rose every school morning;
their songs so fundamental
to my higher education.

American Top 40

Hands down, my favorite math class,
bedroom floor, the most comfortable desk;
notebook opened, paying attention
as Casey counts 'em down.

I'll be adding up the hits,
subtracting all the wannabees,
deciphering life's toughest problems,
while Casey charts the steps to success.

Yes, greater than all the other teachers
who knew nothing of my lesser-than life;
week after week, studying with the master:
Casey – who had it all figured out.

This is Serious Business (Ode to Motown)

The guys, sporting colorful plumes,
spinning in the spotlight,
falling to their knees, pleading,
just trying to catch a break.

The girls, gathered around their hope,
whispering their dreams,
suggesting everything,
but giving away nothing.

Oh, how their desires call and respond,
how they offer each other sweet promises;
those of us caught in between
trying to figure out which side to take.

A Love Supreme

There was a time I listened only to them,
their musings about life matching mine:

how the world was an empty place,
and love meant living in shame –
sometimes it took everything you had
                              just to hang on.

Hit after hit,
Diana begging – bargaining – promising,
her girls echoing those desperate pleas,
bass and drums driving her point home.

For a few years I suffered gladly,
my angst picking that needle up
                              and placing me

back in their arms again,
safe in their sad reflections,
happy with nothing but heartaches.

Invasion

From the shoreline of my teens
I watched another dream sink;

you British guys crossing over,
sailing into the hearts of American girls,

easily winning what I could not fathom,
my ship so oddly off course.

They loved your way of talking,
your cockney attitude,

even the boys here followed your lead –
but I stood my ground,

holding onto the hope
that one of you guys from a foreign land

might be as different as me.

The Record Store

Getting there meant dodging the Rough Boys
who knew, too easily, how to upend my life.
So I went the long way,
which would all be worth it,

    when my fingers
        flipped through those discs,
                each 45 hitting the next,
                        like a heartbeat.

And when I found my latest had-to-have,
I paid a dollar and slipped it beneath my coat,
where it covered my heart:

                armor for the walk home.

Friday Nights, Junior High

Stacked on a hi-fi, waiting their turn
                              hit
                            after
                           groovy
                              hit

Possibilities fill a basement rec room
                              new
                           sounds
                            rising

Fast dances got us working up a sweat
                          getting
                            down

Slow songs guarding our mysteries –

                             45s

keeping time between now   and someday.

Sweet Blindness

Three weeks each year, we were family:
distant cousins growing thick
under summer sun, shining
in our campground by the lake.

And when we'd outgrown ourselves,
one of us – nobody remembers who –
hid a few cans of beer in a donut bag
and snuck to the water's edge,

where we sipped the bitter life,
trying on our grown-up laughter,
singing the hell out of this song –
the best part about being drunk, really:

telling the whole world, good and loud,
we had life all figured out.

Mis-Taken

We never had time to listen to all those records
that became, slyly, ours,
                         lifted
beyond the eyes of gossiping salesladies.

              Oh
                    the
                              daring
        and
                    the
          devilment,
                              the
              out
                        of
          character
                        craziness.

Failed at school and sports, we were hell-bent
on chewing through our apron strings,
                                    and spitting out
our mousy ways

'til one day,
caught and lectured,
we were forced to give everything back

              everything but our important guilt.

Three-Minute Lies

How convenient, these 45 rpm melodramas,
just a radio wave or turntable spin away;
little white lies on black-as-mystery vinyl

so easy to hide behind,
with their predictable plots
and appropriate pronouns

which I claim as *my* love and lust,
delivered quite convincingly,
until late at night, bedroom curtain closed –

alone with my truth
of everything these songs can never be.

He Ain't Heavy

The road is long
with many a winding turn
that leads us to who knows where
who knows where...

The first fifty times I sang along
it was just another hit record,
comfortable to sit with awhile
after four or five fast ones in a row.

But something in its words – what *was* it? –
shook my foundation, breaking me open
to a new way.

... It's a long, long road,
from which there is no return;
while we're on our way to there
why not share?

Fourteen years old,
lost in my brotherlessness,
this song extending its hand.

Cass

People still marvel at her voice –
yes, she had quite a contralto –
but what my mind can never shake
was how well *she* could

with all her heft
draped in that psychedelic era,
so fully embodying her music,
while I sat tapping my foot

everything I felt
crammed into the big toe of my awkwardness,
watching someone
who looked like the sore thumb of show business

have the time of her life.

Kindred (Ode to Janis Joplin)

She waits, as the audience welcomes her,
little girl dressed tough for a great big world,
standing stone-still, shackled

'til the band stokes her fire,
her eyes burning through the TV,
drawing me like a magnet
and pulling from my gut

an urgency.
When she grips that mic, goddamn I believe,
believe that every feather dangling from her hair

she'd grabbed from the sky,
having beaten her way on hell-bent wings –
daring me now to grow a pair,
to make off with everything that's mine.

No Secrets

Not just straight boys
propped your album cover on nightstands –
you braless, floppy-hatted, easily grinning.

While they kept undressing your rockin' body,
I was copping a feel of your heart.

Sure, you looked like you had it all,
hooking up with James,
clubbing with the rich and famous,
but all I cared about

was the slow dance I got from your sorrow.

Maybe you *were* put together on album covers,
but it was being inside your falling apart
that really turned me on.

The First Time Ever I Saw Your Face

Dodge Dart packed with classmates,
idling in a deserted state park,
junior prom romances in overdrive.

Roberta's voice drifts from the radio,
her tender pledging of love
feeling as foreign as the far side of this lake,

its endless waters now a siren's song
drawing me to her shore,
where I toe a pledge of my own,

one that would be so easy to fulfill.
"Come," she says, "dive into your confusion,
choke on the waves of your made-up loves,

sink the truth you could never say aloud."

My Seventeen   (another look at Janis Ian's
At Seventeen)

I knew the truth at seventeen
that love would not be meant for me,
just guys who ruled the high school halls
could play its game, like basketball.

The backseat trysts that ended bad,
the ached-for kiss I never had
were just for boys so unlike me,
at seventeen, I came to see.

And guys like me with tender feelings
practiced smiles at bedroom ceilings
and ended up within ourselves,
our truths unshared with someone else,
there'd be no one to hear our plea:
to be a man and love like me –
no, this was not meant to be
at seventeen.

That brown-eyed guy in tight blue jeans
who joined my every nighttime dream,
said: "Come with me and take what's yours,
come find in me what you deserve."

But wouldn't all my so-called pals
laugh at such a fairy tale,
they'd call me freak if they but knew,
if dreams like mine should end up true.

So remember those outside the game
lose the hope and find our shame,
inventing ways to stay at home,
to miss the dance,
to lie alone,
our every wish a wayward scheme –
ending with life undone
at seventeen...

To those of us who knew the hurt,
who skipped the prom, who'd never flirt,
to we who spoke in vague pronouns,
who heard of love, but made no sound.

It was long ago and far away,
the world more fated than today,
when dreams would surely come to be –
except for guys like me
at seventeen.

Someday

Motown sure knew how to jumpstart a song
that had something important to say;
sending me my marching orders
on decisive strings,
plucking out the direction you were heading

and that I must follow.
For we were at the end of an era
and I was hanging on
to my thread of the '60s,
a decade woven by the Beatles, Dylan,
and your Supreme reign.

But your time had come
to break a heart, dividing
the two who stayed behind

and the one who would turn herself
into something new.
And the time had come

to grow up,
so said my fed-up father
and older brother,
time to divide myself

and leave behind the part of me
that thought loving you *was* love;
marching off,
trampling that thread of hope:
Someday We'll Be Together.

My Sweet Lord

Like Easter morning
ascending from the radio,
he'd come to care for all lost souls,

slipping into my emptiness
on slide guitar,
his disciples anointing me with hallelujahs,

offering what the preachers shaming us from pulpits
and the nuns so wrapped up in their calling
could never deliver – but he could:

his voice no longer a Beatle's,
but a high priest's; his grace
something I never had to pray for

to receive.

My Ten Commandments

"When you're weary, feeling small,
when tears are in your eyes
I'll dry them all"

 "Look over yonder, what do you see?
 The sun is a-risin', most definitely.
 A new day is comin', people are changin'"

  "Yes, a new world's coming
  the one we've had visions of...
  coming in peace, coming in joy, coming in love."

   "Come on people now, smile on your brother
   everybody get together,
   try to love one another, right now."

    "We are stardust, we are golden
    and we've got to get ourselves
    back to the garden."

    "Different strokes for different folks
    and so on and so on and scooby dooby dooby
    oh sha sha We got to live together."

     "I said, War, huh, Good God, y'all
     what is it good for?
     Absolutely nothing – say it again!"

"Reach out and touch somebody's hand
make this world a better place,
if you can."

"Think of your fellow man,
lend him a helping hand
put a little love in your heart.

"And when the brokenhearted people
living in the world agree,
there will be an answer, let it be."

Naturally

First paycheck in hand, I stop at Montgomery Ward to buy my
First stereo phonograph record player. At Greco's, I select my
First long-playing album, Carole King's *Tapestry.* At home, my
First listen fills in

> the part of me that's been missing.

College Bound

Car windows wide open,
night air streaming in,
feeling the fullness of summer

and breathing in the beauty
that Seals and Crofts are singing;
treasuring it, for our tomorrows.

> Old enough to know endless fun ends.
> Young enough to wonder
> how we'll survive leaving it all behind.

No one says a word; the song on the radio
playing like a gentle breeze,
soothing the ache that's closing in.

The Stranger

Columbia album centering
song by song expressing
Billy's life blazing.

Dorm room stifling
single window exposing
college life prevailing.

Virgin heart speculating
curious mind exploring
one life, waiting.

My Closer

"Let's leave our underwear on," you insist;
proper girl entangled in my arms, in my
anxiousness. We're lying atop a mattress
in this cold dorm room, caught up in a chill
I just can't shake.

I don't disagree with your demands,
nor do I offer mine, which would be
to end this game I'm sure as hell losing;
certain of what won't happen for me
again.

Tiny Dancer comes on the radio
and you tell me about your last boyfriend,
how his mother died young and how he'd
play this song to hold you close.
Exiting this world

>   and entering mine,
>   I bring your boyfriend along,
>   and, there, he and I hold,
>   closer than close, everything
>   we have lost.

Haven't Got Time for the Pain

Did you realize what you taught me
with your casual reference to this song,
so out of place in Early American Lit,
but right at home in my freshman heart?

Did you know how you carried me
from that stark classroom
back to my hometown, pain in storage,
which I carried back to you,

wise professor, who I now understand
must have carried your own, too,
and you should know, just by mentioning it,
you taught me so much about the humanities.

"You're not a ship to carry my life,
  you are nailed to my love in many lonely nights"

No matter day or night,
from your dorm room window
you watch everyone else's world.
I arrive:

brief distraction
from all you aren't seeing,
drug store package in hand.
With grateful eyes,

heavy from medicated peace,
you accept this gift

and slip into my hand
a lyric, cleanly inked on lined paper,
Elton's *I Need You To Turn To.*
I smile.

College is beginning to feel like home:
where sadness sits the day away,
where sorrow is my only concern,
where love and dependence are the same song.

One Night Only

"Am   I   Blue?

In sweats and T-shirt

Am   I   B-l-u-u-u-e?

on the stage that is my dorm room

Ain't   these   tears

for an audience of one

In   these   eyes

lips synching, hands

Telling   you?"

Beneath the lines
of this Bette Midler song
I hide beneath a truth
                              and the audience responds.
When the song ends

I'm shocked to see   me   in such finery,

so I strip it away   and exit,

never again asking such wonder-full questions.

Repose

Another summer morning of my nineteenth year; another night cocooned on my cool bedroom floor. I reach above, feel for my turntable's arm, place needle to vinyl and hear Janis Ian breathe life into song.

How sweet, those mornings,
safe within my certainty,
unseen in blindingly-bright days
but undeniable in young light.

I lay another moment in the comfort of my wisdom; then rise, again, into my unpredictable world.

side
B

Old Songs
Heard
New

Aretha - *Live At Fillmore West*

Not so much an album
as an invitation to be.

Her voice,
full as flame

burning through my void,
drawing me in among the living

feeling it.
Feeling it.

Finally Feeling It.

Motown Museum

Am I really here?

Wandering the hallways of yestersong,
moving through rooms where they once grooved:

The skinny, spinning Temptations,
the cunningly coiffed Supremes,
those passionate, pleading 4 Tops
and all the others

crowding this living room
— *Their recording studio*, our guide explains —
its coffee tables pushed to the wall,
rugs tucked under couches
and center stage
one
willing
microphone.

I hold back from the tour,
not ready to leave this history-making truth:
How all those Motor Town songs
— that *Sound of Young America* —
rose from this tiny room

and landed atop my turntable,
where they swelled
the small-town borders of my heart.

"What if a person cried so much
their tears made tracks?"
-Smokey Robinson

He Knew

Dylan said it best:
Smokey *was* the '60s greatest poet,

but we only know that for sure
by surviving the decades since,

then retracing his lyrical lines
back to our tears (our home),

where we found comfort in his crying,
always sung from a higher purpose.

His songs were like miracles, really,
how they kept coming, kept finding the hurt,

working it like a salve, so that,
years after they faded, his caring stayed.

Karen

Each song she sang – whether sunny
or rained upon – came shaded blue,
bound by the threads of her burden.

Who could've guessed – with her fresh-faced
beginnings – all that she carried,
her locked-up life turned with a minor key.

Just those of us – weighted by our own
mysteries – heard her for certain,
for we were listening to someone who understood,

long before we had the words to say.

Disco Fever

If it was such a bad idea:
trading a first-year-teacher funk
    for a fraternity all-nighter,
      pulse of Bee Gees fueling,
        bodies sparking friction,

you finding some other guy to combust with,

      then why do I still wake
    in middle-of-the-nights
sweating to an unending song,
standing outside that dance floor
    forever seeking entry?

Taylor-Made

Once I found you
the way I looked at men changed.

You, with your lonesome voice
riding solo into town,
your attention on pain,
on fire and rain.

With you, men could be pensive,
they could sweetly bare their losses,
they could look up at stars
and count their sorrows.

No wonder Everyman who followed
in flesh and blood
has never measured up –
but I keep on looking

lost in my kind of journey,
searching for your kind of James.

"You kissed me and stopped me from shaking"

37 years old,
confident parent,
director of operations,
 and quite a charmer in a crowd of people

now shaking
like this campground's aspen leaves in a fierce storm;
helpless and held by you.

You got more than you bargained for,
prowling for a weekend hookup.
I got less than I dreamed of,
foraging for a first love...

All these years
I've thought of our moment as some
thrown together lean-to you offered,
then abandoned.

So imagine my surprise today,
at the piano, singing this lyric,
swept back to that thicket,
and rising from it,

> my thanks.

Keep the Change

Watching another New Yorker hail a taxi
stirs Harry Chapin's story-song,
long left idling in my youth.

His words keep me company
as I piece together the wrong turns
of another detoured dream.

Thankfully, this story returns one line at a time,
making reality a little less scary,
for I am singing this song as it was meant:

by a middle-aged man, rearview mirror crowded,
scenery littered with regret, and everywhere
those reminders of my one-way loves.

The Beat Goes On

Drawing an apprehensive breath,
I stand beside you, facing the crowd,
ready to wow 'em with this catchy tune:
karaoke keeping us on track.

Family and friends are in the audience
and I feel the importance of their witnessing
me, with a woman again:
big talk in a small town.

But the lyric keeps catching in my throat,
offering comic relief to the crowd and,
to me, some disturbing divine message:
You can't sing what you don't know.

Still, I plow through, true to my warrior spirit,
having fought my way this far in life –
Yes, I can be Sonny to your Cher:
as long as something keeps feeding me my lines.

Fault

I could understand it
when Tina left Ike,
she had enough of rolling out *Proud Mary*
while he kept her chained to his dream.

It made sense when Sonny lost Cher,
John found Yoko,
Mick traded Bianca for Jerry:
people move on...

but I sure took it hard
when James and Carly broke up;
their marriage the sweetest duet,
their babies like lullabies.

For those few years, they had me believing
two people could be so wrapped up in rapture,
could lie together in grooves of vinyl;
history I could never claim as my own

but was sure would always be.

Brother John

Piano-Playing Balladeer
Angry Young Rocker
Showcasing Glitter King

idolized in my teens,
mesmerized through my manhood –
but not until I realized

we were family,
the story of our lives dictated by other men,
did I understand your heart

which beats true at my piano
whenever I take a seat,
our real story pulsating beneath the words.

The Right Song

I'm 40 years late, but I'd like to say
I'm sorry
for trying to turn you into
my special song.

Halfway through our college roommate bike trip,
surrounded by wilderness,
I suggested how deeply right
you were…

We rode the miles and the silence
fueled by shame and bitterness
until we pulled into that diner,

You Are So Beautiful lifting from the jukebox,
Cocker's hardened voice over a too-gentle piano
taking my hand
and slipping into a booth

with me;
alone, to be sure,
but this time pledging love,
to the right song.

Tunesmiths (Ode to Jimmy Webb and Laura Nyro)

Though you had a lot to say
and found catchy ways to phrase it,
we never got to hear your voice.

Instead, others found fame
standing in your spotlight,
offering you to the world.

Come to find out
I was a lot like you,
with truths of my own

but no way to tell them. Funny,
people assume a song is of the singer,
that words only belong to those being heard.

Music Lesson, 1974

On a Dick Cavett rerun
Paul Simon sings a few lines
of a half-written tune.

How strange, his voice alone.

But then he shows us
how to take that song fragment
and move with it.

Unafraid to sound unfamiliar.

Listening back through his music,
from bridges to Graceland, inspires me
to uncover my relinquished lines.

To move on with my song.

A Good Question, 1974

Dick Cavett asked Bowie what I'm sure he thought was an
intriguing question, while we in the audience, sitting so
comfortably in our youth, feigned interest.

What'll you think it'll be like to be 60? 70?

Bowie smiles

        lifts those impossibly-high cheekbones,
        narrows his gaze through outlined eyes,
        works impatient fingers through hair dyed
                a dozen questioning colors

and looks past Cavett   without an answer.

For Me and for Bob Seger

Here's to guys like me —
      the ones with all the questions,
      who felt the fire inside,
      but forever smoldering.

Here's to guys like you —
      who never had a question,
      who were easy with advice
      on how to grab ourselves some night moves.

Here's to guys like me —
      who moved our lips,
      but heard your voice,
      bragging about those Hollywood nights.

Here's to guys like you —
      who pushed against the wind,
      who, decades later, never changed;
      I mean, how could a rock change?

And here's to guys like me —
      who especially loved it
      when guys like you turned the band down low
      and talked your older-brother talk

      daring me to hop a bike
               and roll away;
      whispering your warning
              of autumn closing in.

Both Sides Now, Once Again

Joni revisits her classic song,
voice smoky-blue, like voices get
after too many rides on a Ferris wheel.

She's got us dreaming again,
weaving through her playful clouds,
hungry for her dizzy dancing fairy tales.

But her wise words found young
and long committed to memory
have a way of rattling a settled heart.

It's true – though, for a time
we were certain – I guess we still
really don't know life at all.

Watching a Beatles Video

What makes it hard to hear today
is not that song's eternal beauty:
Paul working his guitar like a troubadour,
his opening lines whispered, like a prayer;
nor is it the strings, circling his melody,
wrapping it like a precious gift.

No, what is most troubling,
at this point of the journey,
is how hard it is to see, again, Paul's face,
tender and lineless,
his clear eyes searching;
barely a single yesterday behind us.

One of John's Dreamers

They were giant cookie cutter shapes of snow

elephants   alligators   grizzly bears

all sliding off a roof; not falling

                              but floating up

Waking from that dream
felt like 1971,
all of us witnessing his vision. So I

imagined

like he would want,
my dream creatures making love with clouds,
spawning a new species of hope, giving

all the people

reason to set down their handheld worlds
and step outside to see

above us only sky

cradling the grandchildren of his dream.

Aquarius, Where Are You?

Remember it wandering in on a flute,
  its drum stirring our innocence,
    offering the window seat for a starry-eyed flight?

Remember the girls pointing out planets,
  the guys tripping over crystal revelations,
    their voices meeting in the heavens, with an invitation:

Are you ready for the dawning?

Who wouldn't have said yes, back then?

And when you knew you couldn't get much higher,
  along came a strung-on singalong, rejoicing sunshine,
    its endless chorus putting all your questions to rest.

But listen to the song today,

hear it with new-millennium ears,
  then gaze out your double-paned windows;
    those questions out there, still circling.

You've Got a Friend

We were tragically young –
falling into each other's lives
from some All-Powerful Force;
teenage misfits, confused by
what our hearts longed for,
finding clumsy ways to get by

like the day we sat together –
Tapestry filling our musty
high school gym – weaving
tissue-paper flowers into
a junior prom palace. Fitting in
was all that mattered

until this song began, the words
instantly ours; like stumbling
onto a foreign land, already
fluent in its language.
You and I sang it softly.
To each other? To ourselves?

The years rolled by; love more,
not less mysterious: anxious attempts
with girl and boyfriends,
troubles away at college,
our own mismatched marriage –
but, always, this song to lean on.

Just yesterday, you called to say

you saw James and Carole in concert
and thought of me, 3,000 miles
and all that pain away; this song
with us on that phone line,
its truth sent by a love
we've come to know.

You've Got a Friend (James Taylor's Version)

Back in college, I learned this story of a radio DJ
who meant to play some top 40 ditty,
but, when he introduced it,

this song came on instead. Minutes later,
a teenager called in
to thank that DJ for his mistake. See, this kid was

killing time,
listening to the radio,
so ready to turn himself off

when this song came on.
I know a little about
that place we can go,

that alone-in-your-bedroom, curtains-closed,
drowning-in-the-truth kind of place –
but I also know a little bit about

how music can rescue us,
how someone like James
can strum a few chords and sing,

with pure voice,
the hope
we could not yet hear on our own.

C S & N

After all these years
their harmony has stayed;
not the way
old nightmares hang on

but the way three guys
found a dream
and thought to share it
as one.

That's why hearing them today
is still good news:
men gathered around a feeling
singing into each other,

never turning away.

Falling Back in Love with *Mustang Sally*

I forgot how simple it can be:
drums tapping into my desire,
guitar picking out a storyline,
saxophone thickening its plot,

and then his voice –
strayed, yes, from Pentecostal sermons –
but testifying nonetheless,
background girls responding.

Who says it's 2014
when I'm feeling 1966:
a schoolboy for the first time,
hell-bent on getting it right.

I Want You Back

October 14th, 1969, up early, cramming.
A new voice barrels out of my radio,
riding one hell of a three-minute song,
but sounding way too young to drive.
Ditching my homework, I hop in.

May 16th, 1983, another night with the TV.
Motown 25 the evening's entertainment;
Michael breaks free from his brothers,
spirit-dancing across the stage,
teaching *Billie Jean* and me a thing or two.

June 25th, 2009, beneath the midday sun.
My son and I out for a walk and,
as only this modern world can attack,
he gets a text that Michael Jackson is dead.
Gotta be his latest circus act, I convince myself.

January 20th, 2014, mid-winter predawn.
Living room lights killed, Jackson 5 CD spinning,
volume up a few notches. Rising from the couch,
shaking off 45 years
                    I dance to his everlasting voice.

You Make Me Feel (Ode to Aretha)

Your song
      for years
      a women's anthem
      today reconceived
         at my piano

Your spirit
      passed
      from mother to daughter
      now embodied
         by a willful son

Your truth
      envied silently
      across gender lines
      finally expressed
         in commanding voice:

I Am Natural

And

I Feel

Liner Notes

page 2: "Raised" references the following singers and their songs: James Taylor and *Sweet Baby James* written by James Taylor, copyright EMI Blackwood Music Inc./Country Road Music Inc. (BMI); John Lennon and *All You Need Is Love* written by John Lennon and Paul McCartney, copyright Sony/ATV Tunes LLC; Simon & Garfunkel and *The Sounds of Silence,* written by Paul Simon, MCA Music Publishing A.D.O. Universal S, Paul Simon Music; Carole King and *I Feel The Earth Move* written by Carole King, copyright ColGems-EMI Music, Inc.

page 3: "American Top 40" is about Casey Kasem, who hosted the American Top 40 radio show from 1970 until 1988 and 1998 until 2004.

page 5: "A Love Supreme" is about Diana Ross & The Supremes.

page 9: "*Sweet Blindness*," is about the song of the same name, sung by The Fifth Dimension, written by Laura Nyro, copyright EMI Music Publishing.

page 12: *"He Ain't Heavy"* references and includes lyrics from *He Ain't Heavy, He's My Brother*, written by Bobby Russell and Bob Scott, copyright Music Sales Corporation. It was recorded by the Hollies in 1969 and Neil Diamond in 1970.

page 15: *"No Secrets"* is about Carly Simon's album of the same name, released in 1972 on Elektra Records.

page 16: *"The First Time Ever Is Saw Your Face"* references the song of the same name, sung by Roberta Flack, written by Ewan MacColl, copyright Stormking, BMI.

page 17: "My Seventeen" was written in response to *At Seventeen*, written and sung by Janis Ian, copyright Mine Music, LTD.

page 19: "Someday" references *Someday We'll be Together* by Diana Ross & The Supremes; written by Jackey Beavers, Johnny Bristol and Harvey Fuqua; copyright EMI April Music, Inc.

page 20: *"My Sweet Lord"* is about the song of the same name, written and sung by George Harrison, copyright Sony/ATV Music Publishing.

page 21: "My Ten Commandments" features partial lyrics from a string of songs released between February 1969 and August 1970: *Bridge Over Troubled Water*, by Simon & Garfunkel, written by Paul Simon, copyright Universal Music Publishing Group; *Crystal Blue Persuasion*, by Tommy James & The Shondells, written by Eddie Gray, Tommy James and Mike Vale, copyright EMI Music Publishing; *A New World's Coming*, by "Mama" Cass Elliott, written by Barry Mann and Cynthia Weil, copyright Screen Gems EMI; *Let's Get Together*, by the Youngbloods, written by Chet Powers, copyright Irving Music, Inc.; *Woodstock*, by Crosby, Still & Nash, written by Joni Mitchell, copyright Crazy Crow Music; *Everyday People*, by Sly & The Family Stone, written by Sylvester Stone, copyright SONY BMG Entertainment; *War*, by Edwin Starr, written by Barrett Strong and Norman Whitfield, copyright Jobete Music, Inc.; *Reach Out & Touch (Somebody's Hand)* by Diana Ross, written by Nick Ashford and Valerie Simpson, copyright EMI Music Publishing; *Put A Little Love in Your Heart*, sung by Jackie DeShannon, written by Randy Myers, Jimmy Holiday and Jackie DeShannon, copyright EMI Music Publishing, Sony/ATV Music Publishing LLC; *Let It Be*, by The Beatles, written by John Lennon and Paul McCartney, copyright Sony/ATV Publishing.

page 23: "Naturally" mentions Carole King's *Tapestry album,* released on Ode Records in 1971.

page 24: "College Bound" references Seals & Crofts and their song, *Summer Breeze,* written by James Seals and Dash Crofts, copyright Faizilu Publishing.

page 25: *"The Stranger"* is about Billy Joel's album of the same name, released on Columbia Records in 1977.

page 26: "My Closer" references the song, *Tiny Dancer*, by Elton John, words by Elton John and music by Bernie Taupin, copyright Dick James Music Limited.

page 27: *"Haven't Got Time for the Pain"* references the song of the same name, sung by Carly Simon, written by Carly Simon and Jacob Brackman, copyright BMG Rights Management.

page 28: "You're not a ship to carry my life, you are nailed to my love in many lonely nights," are lyrics from the song *I Need You to Turn To*, by Elton John, words by Elton John and music by Bernie Taupin, copyright Dick James Music Limited.

page 29: "One Night Only" references and includes lyrics from *Am I Blue*, sung by Bette Midler, written by Grant Clarke and Harry Akst, copyright WB Music Corp.

page 35: "Aretha – *Live At Fillmore West"* references Aretha Franklin's album of the same name, released on Atlantic Records in 1971.

page 37: "He Knew" includes a quote before the poem, which was taken from an interview with Smokey Robinson describing his inspiration for writing *The Tracks of My Tears.*

page 38: "Karen" is about Karen Carpenter.

page 40: "Taylor-Made" is about James Taylor.

page 41: "You kissed me and stopped me from shaking" are lyrics from the song, *Mandy*, sung by Barry Manilow, written by Scott English and Richard Kerr, copyright Universal Music Publishing.

page 42: "Keep The Change" references the song *Taxi*, written and sung by Harry Chapin, copyright Storysongs, LTD.

page 43: "*The Beat Goes On"* references the song of the same name, sung by Sonny & Cher, written by Sonny Bono, copyright Warner/Chappel Music, Inc., Sony/ATV Music Publishing.

page 44: "Fault" mentions the song *Proud Mary*, sung by Ike & Tina Turner, written by John Fogerty, copyright Concord Music Group, Inc.

page 45: "Brother John" is about Elton John.

page 46: "The Right Song" references the song *You Are So Beautiful*, by Joe Cocker, written by Billy Preston and Bruce Fisher, copyright Irving Music, Inc. and Almo Music Corp.

page 47: "Tunesmiths" honors songwriters Jimmy Webb and Laura

Nyro. Webb wrote such songs as *Up, Up & Away* (the Fifth Dimension); *The Worst that Could Happen* (The Spiral Staircase); *Wichita Lineman, Galveston, By the Time I Get to Phoenix,* (Glen Campbell). Nyro wrote *And When I Die* (Blood, Sweat & Tears); *Stoney End* (Barbra Streisand); *Stoned Soul Picnic, Wedding Bell Blues,* (The Fifth Dimension).

page 51: "*Both Sides Now,* Once More" references the song *Both Sides Now,* written and sung by Joni Mitchell, copyright Siquomb Publishing Company. Joni rerecorded the song in 2000.

page 54: "*Aquarius,* Where Are You?" references the song, *Aquarius/ Let the Sunshine In,* by The Fifth Dimension, from the Broadway musical, *Hair,* words by James Rado and Gerome Ragni, music by Galt MacDermot, copyright EMI Music Publishing.

page 55: "*You've Got A Friend*" references the song of the same name, written and sung by Carole King, from her album, *Tapestry,* copyright Colgems-EMI Music, Inc.

page 57: "*You've Got A Friend* (James Taylor's Version)" references the song *You've Got A Friend,* sung by James Taylor, written by Carole King, copyright Colgems-EMI Music, Inc.

page 58: "C S & N" is about Crosby, Still & Nash.

page 59: "Falling Back in Love with *Mustang Sally*" references the song *Mustang Sally,* by Wilson Pickett, written by Bonny Rice, copyright Springtime Music, Inc. & Fourteenth Hour Music, Inc.

page 60: "*I Want You Back*" references the song of the same name, sung by the Jackson Five, written by The Corporation, copyright Jobete Music Co. Inc/EMI Music, and the song *Billie Jean,* written and sung by Michael Jackson, copyright Mijac Music.

page 61: "*You Make Me Feel* (Ode To Aretha)" references the song *You Make Me Feel (Like A Natural Woman),* written by Carole King and Gerry Goffin, copyright Screen Gems-EMI Music, Inc., sung by Aretha Franklin.

back cover: "Ways Back" features titles of the following songs: *Red*

ACKNOWLEDGEMENTS

Many thanks for the support I received
as my dream for this book became a reality.

My Critique group:
    Joe Abbate
    Lisa Davis
    Diane Sokolowski

Kathy Andolina
The CNY Arts Center
Carolyn Dougherty
The Downtown Writers Center
Fulton Public Library
Heather and Leah Griffin
Wendy Kaplan
June MacArthur
Alicia Mathias
Maureen Moriarty
the river's end bookstore
Geri Seward
Mary Slimmer
Jim Sokolowski

ABOUT THE AUTHOR

Jim Farfaglia, a native of Central New York, loves being a poet, local-history writer and editor. He has previously published two books of poetry: *Country Boy*, a testimonial to his farming family and rural roots, and *People, Places & Things: The Powerful Nouns of My Life*. His poems are featured in Fulton's *Valley News* and have appeared in *Farming Magazine, The Garden & Farm Almanac,* and in several literary anthologies. Jim is also the author of *Of the Earth: Stories From Oswego County's Muck Farms,* the co-author of *Camp Hollis: The Origins of Oswego County's Children's Camp* and the editor of *Harvest, I Live As a Cloud* and *Fulton: The Stories From Our Past That Inspire Our Future*. Jim maintains a website at www.jimfarfaglia.weebly.com.

18347482R00052

Made in the USA
Middletown, DE
04 March 2015